My
First
Book of
Nature

# Mammals

Victoria Munson

WINDMILL
BOOKS

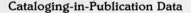

Published in 2019 by Windmill Books,
an Imprint of Rosen Publishing
29 East 21st Street, New York, NY 10010

Copyright © 2019 Wayland, a division of
Hachette Children's Group

Editor: Victoria Brooker
Book Design: Elaine Wilkinson

Photo Credits:
All images and graphics: Shutterstock: Cover:
(main image) Eric Isselee: (tr) oligo; (mr) Jirovo;
(br) Erni; (tl) Matthijs Wetterauw; (bl) Rudmer
Swerver; 1, 3b, 10 Leena Robinson; 2t, 21t David
Osborn; 2b, 9 Martin Prochazkacz; 3, 12t, 12b
Rudmer Zwerver; 4 Andrea Izzotti; 5m Nigel
Dowsett; 5b Ittai; 6 Mirko Graul; 7m Mikhail
hoboton Popov; 7b juefraphoto; 8 Volodymyr
Burdiak; 8m Mark Caunt; 10m Inge Jansen; 11
Pavel Krasensky;13 Erni; 14 Michael G. Mill; 14b
seawhisper; 15 scooperdigital; 16 Carl Mckie;
17t, 17b Erni; 18 Bildagentur Zoonar GmbH; 19t
Erni; 19b Guido Bissattini; 20 Holly Kuchera;
21b LFRabanedo

Cataloging-in-Publication Data

Names: Munson, Victoria.
Title: Mammals / Victoria Munson.
Description: New York : Windmill Books, 2019. |
Series: My first book of nature | Includes glossary
and index.
Identifiers: LCCN ISBN 9781508196167 (pbk.)
| ISBN 9781508196150 (library bound) | ISBN
9781508196174 (6 pack)
Subjects: LCSH: Mammals--Juvenile literature.
Classification: LCC QL706.2 M86 2019 | DDC
599'.03--dc23

Manufactured in the United States of America

CPSIA Compliance Information: Batch #BS18WM:
For Further Information contact Rosen Publishing,
New York, New York at 1-800-237-9932

# Contents

# What Is a Mammal?

A mammal is an animal that breathes air, has a backbone, and can produce milk to feed its young.

All mammals have hair at some stage in their life.

Some mammals, such as cows and horses, are active in the daytime. Nocturnal mammals, such as bats and badgers, are active at night.

Mammals live in many different habitats, such as forests, mountains, deserts, and in or near water.

Polar bears and penguins live at the cold poles.

Most mammals have teeth.

Mammals are found all over the world.

Camels and hyenas live in hot deserts.

5

# Hedgehogs and Moles

Hedgehogs have pointed spikes all over their bodies. An adult hedgehog has about 6,000 spikes.

When hedgehogs feel in danger, they roll themselves up into a spiky ball.

Hedgehogs are nocturnal, which means they sleep in the day and look for food at night.

6

In fall, hedgehogs hibernate.

They dig a small hole and cover themselves with leaves.

When it is warmer in spring, they come out again.

Moles have black, velvety fur. They spend most of their lives underground.

Moles like to eat worms and insects.

Their strong curved front paws are good for digging.

# Badgers and Foxes

Badgers have a black and white striped face. They live in tunnels underground called setts. Badgers have sharp claws that help them to dig.

They sleep in the day and come out at night to feed.

Badgers are omnivores, which means they like to eat meat such as worms or small animals, and plants such as fruits and roots.

Foxes have red-orange fur with white bellies and a bushy tail.

Foxes live underground in dens.

A male fox is called a dog. A female fox is called a vixen. Young foxes are called cubs, pups, or kits.

Foxes have large ears to help them hear mice or voles, which they love to eat.

# Rabbits and Hares

Rabbits are brown with pointy ears and a white tail. They live in burrows underground. They eat grass and tree bark.

When frightened, rabbits will thump their back legs on the ground.

A male rabbit is called a buck. A female rabbit is called a doe.

Hares are bigger than rabbits and have much longer ears and legs. Hares live aboveground.

Jackrabbits are the largest hares in the United States.

Hares can run 45 mph (75 km/h).

Hares eat grass, berries, and tree roots.

Young hares are called leverets.

# Mice and Rats

Wood mice have golden-brown fur and large ears. They live in underground tunnels in fields, gardens, or backyards.

Wood mice eat insects, grasses, berries, and fungi.

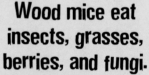

Mice are good at climbing, jumping, and swimming.

House mice have gray-brown fur and large ears. They live near humans, in tunnels under gardens or near houses.

House mice and rats will eat any old food that has been left lying around.

Rats have dark gray fur and a thick, scaly tail. Their tail helps them to balance.

Rats like to live in groups. A group of rats is called a mischief.

# Squirrels

Gray squirrels have gray fur and a bushy tail that is as big as their body.

Red squirrels are reddish-brown, with a bushy tail and large tufted ears.

Squirrels don't hibernate, but they can sleep for days at a time.

Squirrels eat nuts
and berries. In fall,
they bury the nuts and
seeds so that they can
eat them in the winter.

They use their long
claws to open nutshells.

Squirrels'
tails help them to
balance

as they jump from tree to tree.

# Voles and Shrews

Field voles live in the countryside and are very common. They look like mice but are fatter and have a shorter tale.

Voles live in tunnels underground.

They eat plant roots and bulbs.

Water voles have dark brown fur, small ears and eyes, and a short tail.

Water voles are good swimmers.

Water shrews have dark gray fur that looks silvery when it is wet.

Voles and shrews don't live long lives because they have many predators, such as foxes, weasels, and birds of prey.

17

# Stoats and Weasels

Stoats have long, thin bodies. They have orange-brown fur on their backs, white bellies, and a black tip at the end of their tail.

Stoats are carnivores. This means they eat meat such as rabbits, birds, and even foxes.

Young stoats and weasels are called kittens.

18

Weasels look like stoats but are a bit smaller. They don't have a black tip on their tail.

A group of stoats or weasels is called a caravan.

The weasel's slender body helps it to hunt voles and shrews in their burrows.

Stoats and weasels are very good at **climbing.**

# Deer and Elk

White-tailed deer have brown fur. The babies have white spots on their backs.

Baby deer are called fawns.

Deer eat tree shoots and leaves, grass, nuts, and berries.

Elk are related to deer, but they are much larger. Male elk are called bulls. They have antlers that can grow 4 feet (1 m) tall!

The antlers fall off in winter and grow back in spring.

Deer are herbivores, which means they eat only plants.

# Follow That Footprint

Sometimes it's hard to spot animals. Find out if a mammal has been nearby by looking for clues.

*In soft mud, animals will leave footprints behind.*

Look at these footprints and see if you can spot any in your local wildlife habitat.

Fox

Rabbit

# Glossary and Index

**carnivore** an animal that eats mainly meat

**habitat** the natural environment in which an animal or plant usually lives

**herbivore** an animal that eats only plants

**hibernate** to spend the winter sleeping

**omnivore** an animal that eats meat and plants

**predator** an animal that hunts, kills, and eats other animals